The Lifetime Between

The Lifetime Between

Nikki Merriman

Published by Tablo

Dedication

For Joe, my best friend.
Thank you for the courage to find my voice and to put these words to paper; without you, there would be no book—even if you don't know it. Thank you for being the refuge in every storm and the consistency in an ever-changing life. Thank you for always being on my side, even when I'm wrong. I'd be lost in this world without you. Of all the people to have by my side, I'm glad God gave me you. I hate you.

For Clayton, my first real love.
Thank you for changing the way I see myself and the world. Thank you for loving me—for meeting me at my worst back in 2015 and reminding me that I am capable and deserving of love. You've never stopped being one of my number one supporters in all that I do, and my appreciation for you is endless. Thank you for being the soul that helped shape this multi-lifetime approach to love; wherever life takes us, I'll be with you always.

Prologue

Ever written a letter you never sent? Words you've never said but wanted to? Well, that's what you're about to read. Every word, every page, is a note, a letter, a thought to someone specific—a friend, a lover, an ex-lover, a family member, myself. Words left unsaid. Words I was too afraid to say. Words that didn't come until it was too late. Words of hurt, of anger, of love, of hope, of strength. Words of truth—which sometimes hurt.

One day, I came across an old notebook as I was cleaning; inside were many remnants of from a dark time in my life. So, I flipped to the first empty page and started writing again for the first time in years. What was intended to be three or four pages just to get it all out eventually filled the pages of that old notebook and became my first ever publication. That very first day, I had no intention of writing a book, much less publishing one; it's funny how life works. This book is the product of two years worth of breaking open my soul, dealing with the previously ignored pain, and finding those words—finding that truth.

When reading the pages that follow, some will know exactly what I'm talking about. Some will be reading a very personal account of their impact on my life. Some will read these pages and think of themselves or of others. Some will be hopeful, inspired, relieved. Some will be angry, resentful. But, as one of my favorite quotes from Anne

Lamott says, "You own everything that happened to you. Tell your stories. If people wanted you to write warmly about them, they should have behaved better."

The back of this old notebook once held
budgets
cake designs
and wedding vows that promised to keep you safe
in a zombie apocalypse.

Little did I know that I was the zombie
and you were the
apocalypse—
changing me forever,
destroying life as I knew it,
and leaving nothing but chaos in your path.

—a narcissist will never have the cure

It would be an honor
to spend my forever with you.

In a past life you must have been
an acrobat
or a magician
the way you come back without warning,
twist my life up,
throw it for a loop,
and leave
once again
without a trace.

—you know not the harm you've caused

That's the thing about having a spine.
It holds you up—
not everyone else.

All I've known
is the need to stand up for myself.

I do not know how to handle someone being on my side.

I do not cower from my strength,
and neither will the right person.

Never allow loneliness
to become weakness.

—this too shall pass

The right person
will not fear your strength.

The only place I want to be
is next to you.

Quiet.
Peace.
Serenity.
Skin
and blue eyes
and a heartbeat I could listen to forever.
A rare moment of
clarity
and certainty
in a crazy, uncertain world.

These are the moments
I know I will cling to.

You
are my favorite thing about this world.

It's a wonderful thing
for a love to be both
old
and
new
at the same time.

I am yours at 4 AM
When we're tangled up in blue eyes and heartbeats
When the world is still
Except for your hand in my hair—
When goodbye seems so far away.

I am yours at 4 PM
When we're tangled up in reality and responsibility
When the world is loud
And my hand can't reach yours—
When hello seems so far away.

—I'm always yours

I cannot wait
until every 3 AM
is spent with you.

—someday forever

It's you.
It's always been you.

—when you know, you know

I'm terrified.

But nothing good can come out of staying in one place just because of fear.

You've told me that all along.

—I'll never tell you, but you were right

The little things
aren't actually little at all.

Cling to them.

—you

Reality is coming quickly,
and I have yet to learn how to miss you.

—USMA

d i s t a n c e

is only as
permanent
or as
temporary
as you make it.

—no excuses

1 (800) 273-8255

I wish I'd known how to be the light
I didn't even know you needed.

—AB

2 years.
2 seconds.
2 lifetimes.

They're one in the same
since you decided
to go.

—2/15/2017

You held the moon
and when you left,

you didn't even bother to leave the stars.

—the day my world went dark

How wonderful it is
to discover more love—
new love—
in a place where love already grows.

Even the moon slept
as the fire kept watch
and we bared our souls.

Your secrets,
fears,
and insecurities
were now mine,
and mine were yours.

And I knew this would hurt like hell.

Don't apologize for your
scars,
your dents,
your sharp edges,
or your fears.

For the things that remind you you're alive.

For the things that connect me to you.

Every word you said smelled like

g a s ,

and I used every bit of strength I had left
to light a match

and burn this whole thing to the ground.

— *l i g h t i n g*

My soul,
and all the things it's made of,
was a mirror of yours.

So tell me—
what were you really afraid of when you ran?

Life without loving you

No amount of time
could prepare me to watch you love someone else.

This is new territory
that a thousand lifetimes couldn't deem me ready to enter.

So I brace myself
(unsuccessfully)
for the rest of this lifetime,
and pray that
somehow
we get another chance in the next.

How many lifetimes
will it take us to get this right?

—soulmates

What a surprise—
you came out of the blue
and reached out
in an attempt to dust off this old broken heart

And like a break in the clouds,
the break of dawn after a stormy night,
I felt a beat somewhere in its pieces.

—on a scale of 1–10

I'm staring at this blank page
begging for the words to come.
Begging for this book to take the hurt,
if only for a moment.

But this hurt is too strong
for words to break through,
and all I'm getting is tears.
So instead of writing,

I'll cry.

It's just the hurt,
the darkness,

and you.

—another night

And sometimes,
I just cannot stop
the tears from rushing in.

—3 years later

Maybe in the next lifetime,
we'll get it right.

—C

It is a
s l o w ,
infinite,
burning
torture,

to know that you love me.

I never knew the instant,
lingering
taste of regret

until I didn't tell you
I love you.

—see you later

Sometimes,
the hurt is simply
too strong for words.

I try my damnedest.
I fight
I struggle
desperately
to find words to put on this page.

But through these tears,
the only word I can find

is your name.

When will I learn
how to live in this world
when you're not in it?

—no choice

I can't shake this feeling that I should hate you.

But try as I might,
I can't find anything in my soul for you
but love.

The harder I try,
the deeper I dig,
the more impossible love I find.

—unconditional

From day one it's been you.
It's always been you.
I went home three years ago and told my mom I was going to marry you one day.
You've changed my life in ways words cannot describe.

Don't leave.
I'm scared.
I love you.

My god, I'm so in love with you.

—things I should've said

I could tell you that I love you beyond measure,
that I am a better person for knowing you,
that my world is a better place with you in it.

I could also compare the sun to a candle.

—J

Because of you
my sun shines a little brighter,
I walk a little taller,
and I bloom a little fuller.

Because of you,
I am a little more me.

The sun shines on your face,
the birds sing your name in their sweet song,
and the flowers bloom in anticipation of new life ahead.

Your unending love and patience
have sheltered me through every storm.

Your arms have held me above water
through every crashing wave.

And you've never let go.

When the night is dark,
The waves are strong,
And the storm rages on,

I find your face.

—refuge

1 in 3

"But he's never actually hit me!"
screamed my heart.

"He doesn't have to,"
whispered my head.
"And still, he makes it clear he could."

"You've changed, you're such a fucking bitch now."

Yes.
But.

Did the sun stop shining?
Did the moon go dark?
Did the flowers wilt,
or the stars retreat?

Or did I simply say
"No more?"

—enough is enough

And this is never the way
I planned to write about you.

This moment
is standing on a cliff,
on the edge of a forever,
on the brink of an eternity,
on the very tip of incredible change.

But no one talks about
the fear
that is here with me as well
in this moment.

I have done what feels right,
when it feels right,
how it feels right,
and with whom it feels right.

For this I will be questioned,
doubted,
burned at the stake.

For this I will know no regret.

I am an island after a hurricane.
The sun will shine again,
only to illuminate the damage done.

This is trauma.

—category 5 death grip

There are a thousand wonderful words
I could use to describe you.

But
selfless
isn't one of them.

Thank you
for shining your beautiful,
bright,
unconditional,
loving,
earth-shattering light
into the deepest cracks of my concrete soul.

—better

You have always been
that yearned-for light
at the end of the tunnel.

—to this day

I cannot shake the guilt
of not shaking you.

You deserved so much more
than to be tangled up in someone else's red string.

—letting you go

I should be filled with hope—
looking forward to another lifetime with you,
knowing I'll find you again.

—should be

Though the tree comes back as paper,
it will never again be a tree.

—love after you

Love—
real, actual love—
is never lost.

It is simply redefined.

Someday,
you will reap the love you've broken your back to sow.

On nights like these,
our next lifetime seems infinitely far away
(nonexistent)
and the hurt that comes with having to live the rest of this
one without you
is too heavy,
too large,
too great
to even begin to wrap my mind around.

I've spent this entire time
written an entire book
just to try and explain a hurt
that I know in my soul even I'll never be able to
understand
in its entirety.

—no scratches on the surface

I cannot begin to wrap my mind around
loving you
and being loved by you
but not having you.

My mind never wandered
until I tried giving someone else a heart
that I no longer had to give
and would never be able to get back.

You chose me.
You choose me.
That should be enough.

—why isn't it?

Our single fundamental difference:

My can,
your can't.

My will,
your won't.

My "I love you"
and your "but."

—"but" nothing

No force of nature could've stopped me from trying,
nothing in the world could change
the fact that I chose (choose) you,
and there was no excuse legitimate enough
that it would've had any bearing
over the life we both know (knew) we want(ed).

—fundamental differences

Is it possible to love a person,
a place,
a life
that you never thought you wanted?

—grappling

Simply put,
the idea of going through the rest of this lifetime
without you
is too much,
too big,
too deep of a hurt to bear.

And I do not know how I will do it.

I do not know if I can.

—75 more years to go

And I hope you feel the hurt
that soaks these pages.

It's a constant battle between
"I don't want this life without you in it"
and
"I can't handle this hurt."

—better than nothing

And at the end of the day,
You're still all I want.

—guilt

I knew it was you
when home instantly stopped being four walls
and instead became two arms.

When you look at her
at the end of the day,

I know you see me.

One day,
you'll regret not choosing me,

and I'll regret not waiting.

—again

5:20 AM.
You and the city sleep,
but I can't even close my eyes.
In 10 minutes,
you won't be squeezing my hand in your sleep.
The space between your lips when you dream will close.
The peaceful look on your face will disappear.
I won't hear your heartbeat.
Real life will set back in.

But then,
you awaken just enough to put your hand in my hair,
pull me closer,
and kiss my forehead.

And I cling to this moment—
and to you—
for dear life.

The city lights shine through the windows,
illuminating your face—
my world is frozen in time.

And through the song of the city
and the beating of your heart,
I hear you whisper to yourself.

—how it's supposed to be

And all I want—
so very desperately want—
is to remember this moment.

To remember you.

I would choose you.
Over
and over
and over
and over
again.

You—
Always.
Only.
You.

"I love you"
only counts with
"I choose you."

—all or nothing

Woman.
You have the strength to carry the world—
no—
the universe on your shoulders.

But woman,
don't you know?
You don't have to.

—from one to another

Our town is quiet.
Our house is average.
Our car is used.
Our schedule is routine.
Our relationship isn't perfect.
Our life isn't much.

But it's ours.

—extraordinary

As sure as the sun will rise
after the cruelest storm
and the darkest night,

you will be my forever.

—B

Home

Without you,
the warmest,
calmest,
most beautiful beaches in the world

would not be so.

The quietest whisper from the shakiest voice,
strong enough to stop the entire world in its tracks.

—I love you

At last,
my tired bones can rest in your soul.

I should've known
these pages would bleed your name.

Sweet girl,
reach out your arms—

Do you see the world at your fingertips?
Do you feel the stars in your palms?

Beautiful girl,
never stop reaching.

Fear
is no life to live.

You love me.
You want me.
You choose me.

Or you don't.

—no buts

I promise
I will find you in every lifetime.

I will search for you
endlessly.

And I will love you with the same
life-changing love
that I have loved you with

since the beginning of time.

—soulmates / next time

Every lifetime, my love, I will love you infinitely more.
Just like I have from the beginning of time.

One day,
the sun will set for the very last time
and I'll find myself standing
at the edge of the universe,
in a moment between this life and the next.

And in that moment,
I'll turn around
and reach for you.

—waiting

Your ending
was the birth of my beginning.

Your soul
is the most beautiful beginning my heart has ever bloomed
in.

And just like that,
an ending begins again.

About The Author

Nikki is a runner, dancer, teacher, model, and traumatic brain injury and domestic abuse survivor from the Chicagoland area. When she isn't writing (she handwrites all her poems), she enjoys painting, traveling, and spending time with her family and pets. More often than not, you can find her on the beach or near the water. There are few things she enjoys more than hearing from her readers; you can find her and more of her work on Instagram @nixwrites_.